The Juice Bar

The Juice Bar

Sara Lewis

LAKE PRESS

Notes for the reader
This book uses both metric and imperial measurements.
Follow the same units of measurement throughout: do not
mix metric and imperial. All spoon measurements are level:
teaspoons are assumed to be 5 ml and tablespoons are assumed
to be 15 ml. Unless otherwise stated, milk is assumed to be full
fat, individual vegetables are medium, and pepper is freshly
ground black pepper. The publisher recommends consulting a
doctor or other healthcare professional before embarking on
major dietary changes. The publisher disclaims any liability,
loss or risk that may be claimed or incurred as a consequence
— directly or indirectly — of the use and/or application of any
of the contents of this publication. While the author has made
every effort to ensure the information contained in this book is
accurate and up-to-date at the time of publication, medical and
pharmaceutical knowledge is constantly changing. Pregnant
and breastfeeding women are advised to avoid eating peanuts
and peanut products. Sufferers from nut allergies should
be aware that some of the ready-made ingredients used in
the recipes in this book may contain nuts. Always check the
packaging before use.

The author would like to thank John Lewis for the loan
of the Vitamix liquidizer.

⛵ LAKE PRESS

Lake Press Pty Ltd
5 Burwood Road
Hawthorn VIC 3122 Australia
www.lakepress.com.au

This edition published by Parragon Books Ltd in 2013
Copyright ©Lake Press Pty Ltd, 2019
Created and produced by Pene Parker and Becca Spry
Author and food stylist: Sara Lewis
Photographer: Haraala Hamilton
All rights reserved

First published 2019
Printed in China 5 4 3 2 1
LP19 358

6
The juice bar

80
Energy

12
Kick start

118
Health

46
Rehydrate

154
Detox

The juice bar

A juicer can help transform your health. With sugary cakes, high-salt and high-fat crisps, and ready meals within easy reach, and the ever-growing number of fast-food outlets, it is not surprising that levels of obesity, diabetes, heart disease, food allergies, digestive problems, asthma and eczema are rising. Good health is priceless, so why do we fuel our bodies with such junk and wonder at the results? The secret of good health is to take small steps towards long-term healthy eating. Introducing a delicious juice or smoothie daily can help boost your energy, vitamin and mineral levels and in turn improve the health of your skin, hair, eyes and fingernails, as well as your mood and feeling of well-being.

Health benefits

Health professionals recommend that we eat five 80 g/2¾ oz or more portions of fruit and vegetables per day (about one-third of our total daily food consumption). Yet the average consumption is nearer three portions, with only around 15 per cent of people meeting the target. Studies show that people who eat plenty of fruit and vegetables have a lower risk of developing high blood pressure, heart disease, strokes, obesity and some cancers.

It is estimated that diet is likely to contribute to the development of one-third of cancers. Eating more fruit and vegetables is the second most important cancer-prevention strategy after stopping smoking. Other health benefits include the delay in degenerative eye conditions, improved bone and digestive health and reduced symptoms of asthma.

As juices are made using raw ingredients, their nutritional content is high. Many vitamins and minerals are water-soluble, so are lost when cooked in water, and lots are destroyed by heat. When juiced, fruit and vegetables rehydrate the body and provide nutrients in a form that is easy to digest.

Fresh juices and smoothies energize you and can boost your sporting prowess. Smoothies, made in a blender with the whole, prepared fruit whizzed together, release energy into the body slowly, so can help us avoid the peaks and troughs that may lead to mood swings.

Weight-loss programme

Juices can play a key part in a weight-loss programme. You can kick-start a diet by replacing two meals each day with a juice for just two days. After that, replace one meal each day with a juice. Alternatively, if you usually have a mid-morning high-fat or high-sugar snack, or an evening glass of wine, choose a lower-calorie juice instead.

Juices for the family

We can all benefit from juice, from small kids bringing home colds and viruses, to youngsters battling hormones, exam stress and spots, to stressed-out parents, to grandparents and anyone recovering from illness. When giving juices to kids, if you don't let on what's in each drink you'll be amazed at how many veggies you can sneak into them! Curly kale and broccoli are mild, especially when mixed with naturally sweet apple, pineapple, beetroot or parsnip. The key is to get a good mix of flavours. There are three main ways of making a juice: in an electric juicer, a blender or by using a citrus press.

Electric juicers

Electric juicers have come a long way since the 1980s. You get what you pay for, so shop around and do your homework. If the price sounds too good to be true, then the machine may not have the muscle to do the job properly. Here are the things to consider when buying one.

What kind of juices do you want to make?
If you want to juice a mixture of fruit and vegetables, from root vegetables to broccoli to green leafy vegetables, go for a mid-priced centrifugal juicer. These tall models look a bit like a food processor and have a metal basket with teeth that spin round as you press foods through the chute. The juice is collected in a jug and the debris in a pulp container.

If you want to juice your own wheatgrass and lots of green leafy vegetables, then a masticating juicer is for you. These look a little like a mincing machine and work by crushing fruit and vegetables against a stainless-steel filter with a slowly rotating screw. They take longer to use, are fiddly to clean and the good ones tend to be pricey.

How big is the chute? If you have a big chute, ingredients such as apples, pears and beetroots can be added whole.

How many speeds are there? Two speeds are great: choose low for fleshy fruits and vegetables such as tomatoes, and high for hard fruits and vegetables such as apples.

What about the pulp container? Choose one that is a good size so that you don't have to empty it after you have made just one drink.

Is the machine easy to put together? If it's too fiddly then you won't use it.

Can the machine go in the dishwasher? Okay, so the detachable parts are bulky, and no one is suggesting that the motorized base goes in the dishwasher, but if you are rushing out to work in the morning and want to have a healthy juice, this could save you vital minutes.

Blenders

Blenders vary greatly in motor power, speed settings, jug capacity and price. Some of the more powerful models can crush ice, but not all, so check with your manual before doing this. Their efficiency will greatly affect the texture of your juice, and as many kids and adults hate bits, it might be worth upgrading to a better model if your machine lacks muscle.

For less powerful machines, chop fruit up small, especially pineapples and grapefruits, before blending. Put just a few pieces in the blender to begin with, then add the rest through the gap in the lid while the motor is running. Crush ice before adding, or stir cubes into a finished drink.

Smaller 'personal' blenders with detachable drinking containers can be perfect for making a quick drink. Unscrew the blades and screw on the lid; you don't even need to decant the juice into a separate glass before drinking.

If using a blender, you will need to add liquid in the form of chilled water; rice, almond or soya milk; yogurt or juice. Food processors may be used in the same way, but they can have a bigger bowl so are not always great for single servings.

Hand-held electric wands

These can be used for making blended juices. They are not suitable for blending hard ingredients such as apples and root vegetables, but can work well if you press these ingredients through a juicer first and then whizz the juice up with softer fruits such as berries and grapes.

Citrus press

For the odd orange or lemon, a heavy glass, china or stainless-steel press with a ridged domed top will work fine. Choose one with a pip collector and large moat or attached container to collect the juice. Keen cooks often like a small wooden reamer, but you will also need a little bowl to catch the juice. Also available are chrome-plated free-standing extractors with a hinged arm that presses the fruit down onto the squeezer as the juice feeds down into a chrome cup below. Some food processors come with a citrus juicer attachment, but if you plan to make more than one glass of juice at a time, it might be worth buying a separate electric citrus juicer.

Extra bits of kit

Small vegetable brush or new nail brush to scrub fruit and veg that don't need peeling.

Chopping board, good veg knife and peeler.

Biodegradable food bags; add one to the pulp container when juicing.

Ice-cube trays (unless you have a fridge that makes ice cubes and crushed ice). They are also great for freezing juice.

Choosing fruit & vegetables

As a rule of thumb, if the fruits or vegetables don't look good enough to eat then they are not good enough to juice or blend. It can be tempting to use up that elderly banana or slightly battered pear in a juice, but resist the urge.

Glam up your glass

Citrus twists – cut a thin slice from an orange, lemon or lime, then cut a slit into the centre. Twist the slice and perch it on the glass.

Corkscrews – pare a long, thin strip of zest from an orange, lemon or lime. Wrap it tightly around a skewer, hold for a minute, then slide it off and drape the corkscrew over the glass.

Thin slices of courgette or carrot can be pared from the length of the vegetable using a swivel-bladed peeler. Insert a skewer in two places for a curved boat-shape or roll it up tightly.

Foodie stirrers – try cinnamon sticks, halved lemon grass stems or celery sticks.

Mini-skewers – thread a few pieces of fruit onto a cocktail stick, then rest it on the glass.

Salt or sugar kick – dip the top of the glass in lemon juice, then in salt or caster sugar.

How to use a juicer

Simply prepare fruit and vegetables and press them through the juicer. What could be easier? There's no need to add water, but you can if you wish; it depends on the weather, how thirsty you are and how strong-tasting the juice is.

Root vegetables

Sweet potatoes, beetroots, carrots and parsnips just need a trim and a good scrub. There's no need to peel fresh ginger, just add skin and all. Depending on the width of your juicer chute, you may not even need to cut root veg into pieces.

Wheatgrass

Wheatgrass is difficult to juice unless you have a masticating juicer. It's potent too, so don't try to drink too much in one go. If you juice it on its own, aim to serve just 3-tablespoon shots. Alternatively, stir 1 teaspoon of powdered wheatgrass into your juice; it may not contain quite as much nutrition, but it is easy to use.

Melons

Remove the skin from melons. There's no need to remove the seeds as the juicer can make super-speedy work of separating these.

Citrus fruits

Pare away the zest, leaving some of the pith on as it contains valuable nutrients. (You can leave some of the zest on lemons and limes for a tangy citrus hit if you prefer, but not on oranges or grapefruits.) If you want a thinner drink, squeeze the juice from the fruit before adding it.

Pineapples & kiwi fruits

Remove the skin from pineapples, but there's no need to remove the eyes or core. You can leave the skin on kiwi fruits, but the juice will not look as vibrant if you do.

Best for blending

The blender is best for softer fruits and vegetables. Avocados, tomatoes, bananas, soft juicy berries and seedless grapes all work brilliantly and blitz to a wonderfully smooth drink in a blender. But you will need to add yogurt, or unsweetened soya, almond or rice milk, or a splash of chilled water to help the blades whizz round.

Prepare fruits and vegetables exactly as you would for a salad: remove stones; peel off dark green, furry or knobbly skins; and peel the zest from citrus fruits but leave on some of the pith for extra fibre and a creamy texture. You don't need to skin tomatoes. Peel harder fruits such as pineapples and chop them into small pieces (there is no need to remove the core of a pineapple). Root vegetables, red cabbages, apples and pears are too hard for blending, so must be fed through a juicer before being added to a blender and mixed with softer fruits and vegetables. Seeds and grains are best ground to a fine powder in a blender before you add them to a juice.

Softer vegetables & herbs

Soft vegetables, including lettuce, broccoli florets, cabbage, celery, courgettes, cucumber, kale, tomatoes and peppers, and herbs should be added to the chute between solid vegetables or fruit where possible.

Papayas

Cut papayas in half and scoop out the seeds, then thinly cut the flesh away from the peel. They don't produce much juice.

Apples & pears

Wash apples and pears well, then juice them whole or cut them in half if needed to fit them into the juicer chute.

Mangos

Cut a thick slice off the top and bottom of a mango to reveal the large, flat stone. Cut around this stone, pull away the flesh and cut it from the skin. The fruit doesn't produce much juice, so mix it with melon, apple or pineapple.

Kick start

Muesli motivator

Refreshing and super-zingy, this smoothie makes a delicious energy-packed breakfast. It will keep you feeling full until lunchtime thanks to the natural fruit sugars and slow-release complex carbs from the grapefruit pith, porridge oats and almonds.

Serves 1

* 20 g/¾ oz porridge oats
* 30 g/1 oz flaked almonds
* ½ ruby red grapefruit, zest and a little pith removed, deseeded and roughly chopped
* 150 g/5½ oz raspberries
* 2 oranges, juice squeezed
* 125 ml/4 fl oz chilled water

How to make it

Put the porridge oats and almonds in a blender and whizz until finely ground. Add the grapefruit, raspberries, orange juice and water and whizz until smooth. Pour into a glass and serve.

Nutty facts

Adding 1–2 tablespoons of almonds to a smoothie boosts its vitamin E, B vitamin and protein levels, which is especially good news for vegetarians. Oats contain soluble fibre, and they and the grapefruit pith stimulate digestion and help remove cholesterol from the body.

Make it perfect!
Be sure to cut grapefruit up into small pieces before putting it in your blender so that you get a smooth juice.

Berry breakfast

This breakfast-in-a-glass is packed with sustaining nutrients to keep up your energy levels all morning.

Serves 1

* 200 g/7 oz strawberries
* 100 g/3½ oz raspberries
* 100 ml/3½ fl oz unsweetened rice, almond or soya milk
* 40 g/1½ oz unsweetened muesli

To make this juice

Cut a strawberry in half and reserve one half. Remove the hulls from the remaining strawberries. Put the strawberries and raspberries in a blender and whizz to a purée. Add the milk and muesli and whizz until almost smooth. Pour into a glass, top with the reserved strawberry half and serve.

Sensational strawberries

Strawberries have more vitamin C than any other red berries and so have great antiviral and antibacterial properties. They are rich in beta carotene, which is converted by the body into vitamin A. Their natural fruit sugars also give the body an early-morning energy boost. Strawberries contain lignin, which may help reduce blood cholesterol.

Say yes to soya!

Adding soya yogurt or soya milk to a juice is a great way to boost its protein levels. Many soya milks are fortified with vitamin D and calcium, which means they can also help strengthen bones and teeth. Choose soya yogurt or milk that is unsweetened. They are free from the milk sugar lactose, too.

Nutrient boosters

Fruit and vegetables
are packed with nutrients –
but add a few seeds,
grains or nuts to your juice or
smoothie and it will be
an energy-lifting
protein fix or vitamin
and mineral
power-boost.

Nuts

Bursting with protein, just a
tablespoon of nuts can give a boost to
any fresh juice. Grind them in a blender,
then add fruits and whizz them up or
store them in a jar in the fridge ready
to stir into a juice. They are high in fat,
which bumps up the calories, but they
contain essential fatty acids, are rich in
vitamin E, and include most of the B
group of vitamins and a whole
lot of minerals.

Wheat germ

Wheat germ is the small part inside
a wheat grain, from which a plant
grows. It should not be confused with
wheat bran, which is the outer, fibrous part
of the grain. It is packed with protein to aid
muscle development, vitamin E to boost
immunity and aid skin health, omega-3
fatty acids, zinc, magnesium, some
of the B group of vitamins and
fibre. It is sold as flakes.

Oats

A great source
of energy, oats'
complex carbohydrates
mean that they are
digested slowly and so
help maintain sugar levels
in the blood. Rich in soluble
fibre, they help lower blood
cholesterol levels too. They are
low in fat and a good source
of protein. Grind in a blender,
then whizz with fruit and
vegetables or stir into fresh
juices. They contain avenin,
a protein similar to gluten,
which some
gluten-intolerant
people are also
intolerant to.

Sesame, sunflower & pumpkin seeds

Each of these seeds contains protein, B vitamins, vitamin E and fibre. One tablespoon can contain as many as 100 calories, depending on which seed you choose, so they add an energy boost to drinks. They contain monounsaturated fats (good fats) too!

Ancient Aztecs believed that just 1 tablespoon of chia seeds could sustain a warrior for 24 hours.

Chia seeds

The new seeds on the block, chia deserve a special mention. Just 2 tablespoons can add valuable protein, fibre and omega-3 and omega-6 fatty acids to a drink, not to mention calcium, iron, copper and zinc. They're almost flavourless, so go unnoticed when ground and mixed into a juice. When combined with liquid, they form a gel, so help you feel full for longer.

Flaxseeds & hemp seeds

Sometimes called linseeds, golden or dark flaxseeds are rich in B vitamins, magnesium, manganese, and omega-3 and omega-6 fatty acids. They are also high in fibre and phytochemicals, including antioxidants (although these are not found in the oil). Hemp seeds are the only seeds that contains all essential amino acids, so are a great source of protein.

Power-boosting beets

This robust, vibrant-coloured juice is packed with big flavours and energy-boosting nutrients to get you going in the morning.

Serves 1

* 2 beetroots, halved
* 2 large carrots, halved
* 2 celery sticks, halved
* 5-cm/2-inch piece of cucumber
* 2 red-skinned apples, halved
* 30 g/1 oz walnut pieces, finely ground
* small handful of ice (optional)

Whizz it up

Cut two wafer-thin slices off one of the beetroot halves and reserve. Feed the beetroot and carrots, then celery and cucumber, then apples through a juicer. Stir in the walnuts. Half-fill a glass with ice (if using), then pour in the juice. Thread the beetroot slices through a cocktail stick, lay this on top of the glass and serve immediately.

Sweet beetroot

Beetroot has one of the highest sugar levels of any vegetable, with the equivalent of 1 teaspoon of natural fruit sugar in each 115 g/4 oz portion, so it gives a great energy boost. It also contains folates, vitamin C and potassium, which help to regulate blood pressure and nerve function.

Beat the morning blues

Full of vitamin C-packed berries, this hearty juice is a truly supercharged breakfast immunity boost!

Serves 1

* 1 pear, halved
* 150 g/5½ oz blueberries
* 100 ml/3½ fl oz soya yogurt
* ½ tsp agave syrup
* 2 tsp flaked almonds, toasted

Give it a whirl

Feed the pear through a juicer. Pour the juice into a blender, add the blueberries and whizz. Add the yogurt and agave syrup and whizz again until smooth. Pour into a glass, sprinkle with the almonds and serve.

Agave syrup

The succulent agave plant, which is related to the yucca and lily, grows in the southern and western United States and in tropical South America. Agave syrup, extracted from agave plants, is sold in health-food shops and is used as a sweetener. It is considered by many to be superior to sugar because, when compared with other sweeteners, it has a low-glycaemic index, which means that it won't cause a sharp rise or fall in blood sugar when eaten.

Health notes

Our bodies need protein, which is found in almonds and soya yogurt, for the growth and repair of everything from muscles and bones to hair and fingernails. There's calcium and vitamin D in some fortified brands of soya yogurt too. This breakfast-boosting drink also provides the minerals phosphorus, magnesium and zinc, which are great for our bones and teeth.

Berry kick-start

This energizing, gorgeous-looking smoothie is a delicious and healthy way to kick-start your day.

Serves 1

* 175 g/6 oz blueberries
* 115 g/4 oz cranberries
* 150 ml/5 fl oz natural yogurt
* 2 tsp clear honey
* 4 tbsp chilled water

To make this juice

Put the blueberries and cranberries in a blender and whizz until smooth. Add the yogurt, honey and water and whizz again. Pour into a glass and serve.

Don't fancy honey & sugar? Try these...

Honey supplies energy in the form of simple carbohydrates and is a mixture of fructose and glucose. The clearer the honey, the higher the fructose level. Sweet foods stimulate the brain to produce endorphins, the body's natural pain killers. Agave syrup, brown rice syrup and date syrup can all be used instead of honey. Agave syrup is naturally sweeter than honey. Brown rice syrup has a mild caramel flavour and is like maple syrup. Date syrup is a thick, concentrated purée of lightly cooked dates; you can make it by gently simmering dates with a little water, cinnamon and vanilla, then puréeing and storing in the fridge.

Superfood: blueberries

Blueberries are packed with more antioxidants than many other fruits and vegetables. These antioxidants, called flavonoids, help to mop up damaging free radicals and help to protect the body from premature ageing, heart disease, cancer and degenerative diseases. Forty blueberries (80 g/2¾ oz) contain seven and a half times more antioxidant activity than a small banana. They also contain vitamin C, which our body needs daily, natural fruit sugar for energy, and pectin, thought to help lower cholesterol and act as an anti-inflammatory.

Strawberry supercharge

The pomegranate is one of the oldest cultivated fruits and has been thought to symbolize health, fertility and eternal life. This drink may not give you eternal life, but it will give you a supercharged vitamin boost to help you cope with the stresses of the day.

Serves 1

* 225 g/8 oz strawberries, hulled
* ½ large pomegranate, seeds only
* 2 apples, halved
* small handful of crushed ice (optional)

Give it a whirl

Feed the strawberries, pomegranate seeds and apples through a juicer. Half-fill a glass with crushed ice (if using), then pour in the juice and serve immediately.

Apples for concentration

After intense concentration at work or physical exercise, energy levels plummet. Apples provide natural sugars, which are more slowly absorbed than sugars found in manufactured glucose-rich energy drinks.

Green giant

Gently wake up with this gorgeous, velvety-smooth, soothing juice. Think of it as a hug from the inside out! It looks and tastes good, and is packed with vitamins A, B, C and E, plus the minerals iron and potassium.

Serves 1

* 1 apple, halved
* 30 g/1 oz green curly kale
* 2 kiwi fruit, peeled
* 2 stems of fresh flat-leaf parsley
* ½ avocado, pitted and flesh scooped from the skin
* 4 tbsp chilled water
* small handful of crushed ice

To make this juice

Feed the apple, then kale and kiwi fruit through a juicer. Pour the juice into a blender, add the parsley and avocado, and whizz. Add the water and crushed ice and whizz again, until smooth. Pour into a glass and serve immediately.

Green giant
page 29

Strawberry supercharge
page 28

Ready, steady, go!

Breakfast is arguably the most important meal of the day, and this shake includes lots of vital nutrients. It's quick to make, tasty and filling, but won't leave you feeling heavy.

Serves 1

* 20 g/¾ oz pumpkin seeds
* 20 g/¾ oz flaxseeds (linseeds)
* 20 g/¾ oz oz flaked almonds
* 115 g/4 oz raspberries
* 115 g/4 oz blueberries
* 225 g/8 oz vanilla soya yogurt
* 125 ml/4 fl oz chilled water

Mix it up

Put the pumpkin seeds, flaxseeds and almonds in a blender and whizz until finely ground. Add the raspberries, blueberries, yogurt and water and whizz until smooth. Pour into a glass and serve.

Quick banana boosters

Need to grab a quick breakfast? Then try these fab banana-based energy drinks. They're super-quick, super-simple and super-healthy!

1 Banana & blueberry

* 1 banana, peeled and roughly chopped
* 115 g/4 oz blueberries
* 125 ml/4 fl oz unsweetened rice milk
* small handful of crushed ice

2 Banana & kiwi

* 1 banana, peeled and roughly chopped
* 2 kiwi fruit, peeled and roughly chopped
* 125 ml/4 fl oz unsweetened rice milk
* small handful of crushed ice

3 Banana & mango

* 1 banana, peeled and roughly chopped
* ½ mango, pitted, peeled and flesh roughly chopped
* 125 ml/4 fl oz unsweetened rice milk
* small handful of crushed ice

Serves 1

For each drink, put all the ingredients in a blender and whizz until smooth. Pour into a glass and serve immediately.

Happiness is... a banana!

Feeling a bit down? Forget about chocolate, munch on a banana instead! It is the only fruit to contain the amino acid tryptophan plus vitamin B6, which together help the body produce serotonin (the natural chemical that helps to lift your mood). Naturally rich in fruit sugar and starch, bananas are great energy-boosting foods and have a high amount of potassium. They can help to regulate blood pressure, lower the risk of heart attacks and strokes and reduce the risk of cancer.

Blackberry blaster

Banish those morning blues with this cinnamon-spiced, dairy-free juice. It's bursting with vitamins and minerals, and will keep you energized until lunchtime.

Serves 1

* 3 large red-skinned plums, halved and pitted
* 40 g/1½ oz red curly kale
* 1 pear, halved
* 115 g/4 oz blackberries
* 20 g/¾ oz wheat germ
* pinch of ground cinnamon (optional)
* small handful of crushed ice
* 4-6 tbsp chilled water

Time to get started

Feed the plums, then kale, then pear through a juicer. Pour the juice into a blender. Add the blackberries (reserving one to decorate), wheat germ, cinnamon (if using) and crushed ice, and whizz until smooth. Add the water to taste and whizz again, until smooth. Pour into a glass. Thread a blackberry through a cocktail stick, add it to the glass, and serve immediately.

Blackberries: nature's aspirin

Energy-boosting blackberries are a good source of vitamin C, folates and fibre. More unusually, they also contain salicylates, a natural aspirin-like compound, so if you are allergic to aspirin steer clear of this fruit.

Vegetable tummy treat

Wake up your body and stimulate your digestive system with this fresh-tasting orange-and-tomato drink. There is also a kick in the tail delivered by the chilli, to shake up those taste buds!

Serves 1

* 3 oranges, zest and a little pith removed
* 1 carrot, halved
* 2 tomatoes, roughly chopped
* 125 ml/4 fl oz chilled water
* 1 small green chilli, halved
* 2 celery sticks, thickly sliced
* 2 tsp hemp seed oil

Give it a whirl

Cut 2 oranges in half and feed them and the carrot through a juicer. Pour the juice into a blender. Roughly chop and deseed the remaining orange, then put it, the tomatoes and water in the blender and whizz until smooth. Add the chilli and celery and whizz again until blended. Pour into a glass, stir in the hemp seed oil and serve.

Hurray for hemp seed oil

Hemp seed oil contains a good balance of both omega-3 and omega-6 fats. The Department of Health finds that it is the balance of these fats that is most important in maintaining health and protecting us from disease.

Carrot & ginger vitamin vitality

You don't need a partner for this kind of passion, just a couple of juicy passion fruit! Their delicately perfumed seeds add a touch of luxury to this otherwise simple juice. The fruits were originally called 'grenadilla', but were renamed by Catholic missionaries, who thought their flowers looked like the crown of thorns that was placed on Christ's head.

Serves 1

* 3 large carrots, halved
* 2 passion fruits, seeds scooped out
* 1-cm/½-inch piece of fresh ginger
* 2 apples, halved
* 2 tsp wheat germ oil
* small handful of ice (optional)

Give it a whirl

Feed the carrots, then passion fruit seeds, then ginger, then apples through a juicer. Stir in the oil. Half-fill a glass with ice (if using), then pour in the juice and serve immediately.

Passion fruit power

The more wrinkled a passion fruit is, the sweeter the pulp will be. Each fruit contains up to 250 seeds packed into a juicy, aromatic sweet-sour yellow pulp that contains calcium, iron and vitamins A and C.

Peachy wake-up call

The sweet potato works brilliantly with the sweetness of the peach and fiery punch of the ginger, a fab way to shrug off early morning sluggishness!

Serves 1

* 1 sweet potato, cut into 4
* 1-cm/½-inch piece of fresh ginger
* 3 carrots, halved
* 3 peaches, halved and pitted
* small handful of ice (optional)
* pinch of ground mixed spice, to serve (optional)

Give it a whirl

Feed the sweet potato and ginger, then carrots, then peaches through a juicer. Half-fill a glass with ice (if using), then pour in the juice. Sprinkle with the mixed spice (if using) and serve immediately.

Peachy
wake-up call
page 39

Carrot & ginger
vitamin vitality
page 38

Tropical sunrise & shine

Cheer up the dullest morning with this tropical fruit blend, and ramp up its nutrition with a sprinkling of chia seeds. If you're in a hurry, pack the juice into an insulated flask and enjoy it instead of a caffeine-loaded tea or coffee when you get to work.

Serves 1

* 20 g/¾ oz goji berries
* 15 g/½ oz chia seeds
* ½ papaya, peeled, deseeded and roughly chopped
* ¼ pineapple, peeled and roughly chopped
* ½ lime, zest and a little pith removed, deseeded and roughly chopped
* 225 ml/8 fl oz chilled water
* small handful of crushed ice (optional)

Bring me sunshine!

Put the goji berries and chia seeds in a blender and whizz until finely ground. Add the papaya, pineapple, lime and water and whizz until smooth. Add the crushed ice (if using) and whizz again, until blended. Pour into a glass and serve immediately.

Mango magic start-up

This beautiful smoothie is packed with powerful heart-protective and cancer-fighting antioxidants, plus vitamins B and C. Mangos, oranges and pomegranate seeds are all good sources of potassium, which helps to regulate blood pressure.

Serves 1

* ½ pomegranate, seeds only
* 1 mango, pitted, peeled and roughly chopped
* 1 orange, zest and a little pith removed, deseeded and roughly chopped

Go, man, go!

Reserve 1 tablespoon of the pomegranate seeds. Put the rest in a blender and whizz until combined, then pour into a glass. Put the mango and orange in the blender and whizz until smooth. Pour onto the pomegranate juice, sprinkle with the reserved pomegranate seeds and serve.

The power of pomegranate

It only takes a few minutes to pop the pomegranate seeds from the fruit, but they are nutrient-dense and contain high levels of flavonoids and polyphenols, potent antioxidants thought to help protect against heart disease and cancer. It's claimed that a glass of pomegranate juice contains more antioxidants than red wine, green tea, blueberries and cranberries.

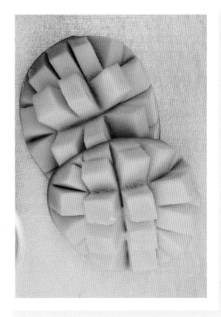

Red rouser

Get the day off to a fabulously fruity start with this irresistibly zingy and pretty juice!

Serves 1

* 1 apple, halved
* 350 g/12 oz cherries, pitted
* 100 g/3½ oz red grapes
* ½ lime, zest and a little pith removed, with a wedge to serve
* 2 tbsp soya yogurt

Whizz it up

Feed the apple, then cherries, grapes and lime through a juicer. Whisk in the yogurt. Pour into a glass and serve with a lime wedge.

Gadget tip!

A cherry stoner is small and easy to store – and it makes taking the stones out of the fruit child's play!

Rehydrate

Go, kids, go!

Start giving your kids the healthy-eating message when they are young with these juices. The oranges are squeezed to make the juices extra smooth.

1

Strawberry & banana

* 150 g/5½ oz strawberries, hulled
* 1 banana, peeled and roughly chopped
* ½ orange, juice squeezed
* small handful of crushed ice
* chilled water, to taste

Serves 1

For each drink, put all the fruit and juice in a blender and whizz until smooth. Add the crushed ice and whizz again. Pour into a glass, top up with water to taste, and serve immediately.

Kids' nutrition

Kids need nutrient-dense foods to maintain energy levels and good fats from dairy foods for fat-soluble vitamins that are vital for growing bones and teeth. They need fibre too, but not too much of it or those tiny tummies will fill up before enough protein, vitamins and minerals have been consumed.

2

Avocado & grape

* ½ avocado, pitted and flesh scooped from the skin
* 115 g/4 oz green seedless grapes
* ½ orange, juice squeezed
* small handful of crushed ice
* chilled water, to taste

Choosing a blender

Most kids hate bits, so buy the best blender you can afford. Budget ones don't always make smooth drinks!

Juice benefits

Fruit and vegetable juices are great ways to sneak lots of nutrients into your child's diet without him or her noticing. Serve with a sandwich for a healthy lunch.

3

Carrot & papaya

* ½ papaya, peeled, deseeded and roughly chopped
* ½ orange, juice squeezed
* 2 carrots, halved and fed through a juicer
* small handful of crushed ice
* chilled water, to taste

Tantalizing tomato refresher

The success of this refreshing juice depends on the quality of the tomatoes; home-grown and just-picked ones are perfect, but otherwise choose good, generously sized, deeply coloured ones sold on the vine for the best flavour.

Serves 1

* 2 carrots, halved
* 1 celery stick, halved
* 2.5-cm/1-inch slice of broccoli stem
* small handful of fresh basil leaves
* 4 tomatoes
* small handful of ice (optional)

Juice it up

Feed the carrots, then celery, broccoli and most of the basil, then tomatoes through a juicer. Half-fill a glass with ice (if using), then pour in the juice. Garnish with the remaining basil leaves and serve immediately.

How to juice herbs

To get the most juice from herbs, sandwich them between firmer fruit or vegetables so that their weight helps to press down on the leaves as they go through the juicer chute.

Kiwi quencher

What a combo: cool, jewel-like kiwi fruits blended with naturally juicy green grapes and thirst-quenching lettuce.

Serves 1

* ½ romaine lettuce
* 4 kiwi fruits, peeled
* 115 g/4 oz green grapes
* 1 large pear, halved
* small handful of ice, to serve (optional)

To make this juice

Peel off a lettuce leaf and reserve. Feed the kiwi fruits and grapes, then lettuce and pear through a juicer. Half-fill a glass with ice (if using), then pour in the juice. Decorate with the reserved lettuce leaf and serve immediately.

Superfood: kiwi fruits

A single kiwi fruit contains more immune-boosting vitamin C than the recommended daily allowance and as much potassium as a small banana, helping to maintain fluid and electrolyte balance. They are rich in magnesium, which improves nerve and muscle function while boosting your energy levels, and zinc for healthy hair, skin, teeth and nails. There's lutein too, an antioxidant that seems to protect against macular degeneration (the UK's leading cause of impaired vision in over-50s).

Ruby fruit reviver

There's nothing more refreshing than a locally grown strawberry in the summer, but this smoothie can be enjoyed at any time of year – just shop carefully for the imported strawberries that really smell and taste as they should: biggest doesn't necessarily mean best!

Serves 1

* 1 ruby red grapefruit, zest and a little pith removed, deseeded and roughly chopped
* ¼ cucumber, roughly chopped
* 150 g/5½ oz strawberries, hulled
* small handful of crushed ice (optional)

Great ruby grapefruits

Ruby grapefruits contain lycopene, an antioxidant thought to help protect the body against some cancers and lower the risk of heart disease. They're sweeter than white-fleshed varieties and packed with vitamin C. In this drink, the strawberries also contain antioxidants and vitamin C, plus ellagic acid (which may help protect against collagen destruction and the inflammatory response after sun damage that can cause wrinkles).

Time for a revival

Put the grapefruit and cucumber in a blender and whizz until smooth. Add the strawberries and crushed ice (if using) and whizz until blended. Pour into a glass and serve immediately.

Raspberry & watermelon crush

As the name suggests, watermelon is packed full of water, so what better way to rehydrate your body than with this delicately flavoured smoothie blended with the natural sweetness of raspberries and a hint of lime?

Serves 1

* ¼ small watermelon, peeled, roughly chopped and most of the black seeds removed
* ½ lime, zest and most of the pith removed, deseeded and roughly chopped
* 115 g/4 oz raspberries
* small handful of crushed ice

To make this juice

Put the watermelon and lime in a blender and whizz until smooth. Add the raspberries and crushed ice and whizz again. Pour into a glass and serve immediately.

Minted melon squash

Quench your thirst with the lightest of fruit squashes. Forget sugar-loaded commercial squashes; this simple home-made one has just four ingredients plus ice and is additive-free.

Serves 1

* ½ honeydew melon, thickly sliced and peel removed
* 5 stems of fresh mint
* ½ lime, zest and a little pith removed
* 2.5-cm/1-inch slice of broccoli stem
* small handful of crushed ice (optional)

Time to get started

Feed the melon and mint, then lime and broccoli through a juicer. Half-fill a glass with crushed ice (if using), then pour in the juice and serve immediately.

Give broccoli a chance

Broccoli is packed with beneficial phytochemicals, including indoles (nitrogen compounds that may help to prevent carcinogens from damaging DNA and so help to protect against cancer). It also contains vitamin C, beta carotene, folate, iron and potassium. The stem has just as many nutrients as the florets, yet it is often binned.

Cherry aid

Fresh cherries taste of pure summer! If you're short of time, use ready-pitted frozen ones, but thaw them in the microwave or leave them in the kitchen for half an hour first, so that you can get the maximum juice out of them.

Serves 1

* 2 pears, halved
* 1 tbsp chia seeds
* 175 g/6 oz cherries, pitted
* 125 ml/4 fl oz chilled water
* small handful of crushed ice (optional)

Mix it up

Feed the pears through a juicer. Put the chia seeds in a blender and whizz until finely ground. Add the pear juice, cherries, water and crushed ice (if using) and whizz until smooth. Pour into a glass and serve immediately.

Cherry baby

Cherries are high in antioxidant properties, which are thought to help protect against cancer. Rich in beta carotene and potassium, they are sometimes known as nature's most powerful anti-inflammatories. Drinking tart cherry juice mixed with water may be beneficial for people with arthritis and gout and has even been linked with improved memory. Now where did I put my keys?

Minted melon squash

page 60

Summer corn quencher

Sweetcorn makes a delicious, creamy, smooth drink. Mix with juicy yellow pepper, naturally sweet apple and a hint of coriander and you have a summer cocktail that will soothe the most parched of throats.

Serves 1

* 1 sweetcorn
* 4 stems of fresh coriander
* 1 yellow pepper, halved
* 1 apple, halved
* small handful of ice (optional)

Whizz it up

Cut the niblets from the sweetcorn, then feed them through a juicer. Feed the coriander, then pepper, then apple through the juicer. Half-fill a glass with ice (if using), then pour in the juice and serve immediately.

Cherry aid

page 61

Dark beet thirst-quencher

Cool down on a hot day with this gorgeous-looking thirst-quencher. The natural sweetness of the beetroot will make it surprisingly tempting for kids as well as adults.

Serves 1

* 1 orange, deseeded and zest and a little pith removed
* 85 g/3 oz cooked beetroot
* 3 tbsp natural yogurt
* 75 ml/2½ fl oz chilled water

Give it a whirl

Remove a segment from the orange, cut it in half and reserve, then roughly chop the rest. Put the beetroot and orange in a blender and whizz until smooth. Add the yogurt and water and whizz again. Pour into a glass. Thread the orange pieces through a cocktail stick, lay this on top of the glass and serve.

Stay hydrated

Water makes up about 70 per cent of our muscles and 75 per cent of our brains. In everyday breathing we lose about 500 ml/18 fl oz water, so it is important to keep the body hydrated all year round rather than just when the weather is hot. When we exercise we lose more water through sweat. Caffeinated drinks such as tea and coffee, or alcohol, all contain substances that cause dehydration.

Cool as a cucumber

This is like a cooling, summer salad in a glass: light and fresh, with a gentle pepperiness from the rocket, a dash of mouth-freshening garden mint and a hint of appley sweetness.

Serves 1

* ½ cucumber, halved
* 15 g/½ oz rocket
* 3 stems of fresh mint
* 1 courgette
* 1 celery stick, halved
* 1 apple, halved
* small handful of crushed ice (optional)

Go cucumber crazy!

Feed the cucumber, then rocket and mint, then courgette, celery and apple through a juicer. Half-fill a glass with crushed ice (if using), then pour in the juice and serve immediately.

Water & your bowels

You need water not only to keep your body hydrated, but also to keep your bowel moving. The longer food waste stays in the colon, the more dehydrated and compacted it becomes and the more difficult it is to shift. Aim to drink at least 1.7 litres/3 pints water each day; fresh juices will count but don't overdo them or your constipation will become quite the opposite.

Celery

Not a fan of celery? Leave it out and add a little more cucumber instead. If you do add it, remember that you can juice the leaves.

Fennel & tomato refresher

Aromatic fennel, fresh celery and tomatoes, a zingy citrus hit and subtly sweet apple – this refreshing drink is great served any time of day or as a light lunch.

Serves 1

* 1 fennel bulb, halved
* 1 apple, halved
* 2 oranges, deseeded and zest and a little pith removed
* 2 celery sticks, halved
* 4 tomatoes
* small handful of crushed ice (optional)

Get ready, get set, go...

Feed the fennel and apple, then oranges and celery, then tomatoes through a juicer. Half-fill a glass with crushed ice (if using), then pour in the juice and serve immediately.

Cool as a cucumber
page 66

Fennel & tomato refresher
page 67

Peach perfect rehydrator

Think of peach melba blended into a foaming fruity drink; perfect on a balmy summer's afternoon. Why not pack this juice into an insulated flask and enjoy it as part of a family picnic or quick lunch for one on a park bench?

Serves 1

* 20 g/¾ oz goji berries
* 2 peaches, halved, pitted and roughly chopped
* 150 g/5¼ oz raspberries
* 225 ml/8 fl oz chilled water
* small handful of crushed ice

For a peach of a drink...

Put the goji berries in a blender and whizz until finely ground. Add all the remaining ingredients and whizz until smooth. Pour into a glass and serve immediately.

Green steam

As melon contains such a high proportion of water, it is great for rehydrating you. Honeydew melon has a light, delicate perfume and flavour. A ripe honeydew should have a bright, lemon-coloured skin, feel firm, but yield slightly when pressed and have no soft spots. Galia and cantaloupe melons would also work well in this drink.

Serves 1

* 85 g/3 oz sugar snap peas
* 5-cm/2-inch piece of cucumber, plus a cucumber stick to garnish
* 2 kiwi fruits, peeled
* ¼ honeydew melon, thickly sliced and peel removed
* 1 tsp spirulina powder (optional)
* 250 ml/9 fl oz chilled water
* small handful of ice (optional)

Give it a whirl

Feed the sugar snap peas, cucumber and kiwi fruits, then melon through a juicer. Stir in the spirulina powder (if using) and top up with the water. Half-fill a glass with ice (if using), then pour in the juice and serve immediately with the cucumber stick as a stirrer.

New to spirulina?

Add spirulina as a protein-booster and watch how it dramatically changes colour from a fine white powder to a cartoon-style dark green. Made from a cultivated algae, it contains chlorophyll, vitamin E, the B group of vitamins, linolenic acid, calcium, iron, protein and zinc. Look out for it in packs in health food shops. (Also see page 122.)

Green
& pleasant juice
Spirulina makes this pea-green
juice turn very dark green.

Melon, pear & ginger spritzer

A refreshingly healthy version of ginger beer, with no chemicals and no added sugars, just 100 per cent natural ingredients.

Serves 1

* ½ honeydew melon, thickly sliced and peel removed
* 1-cm/½-inch piece of fresh ginger
* 1 pear, halved
* small handful of ice (optional)
* 125 ml/4 fl oz sparkling mineral water, chilled

Time for a spritz

Feed the melon, then ginger, then pear through a juicer. Half-fill a glass with ice (if using), then pour in the juice. Top up with the sparkling mineral water and serve immediately.

Berry booster

Think of this juice as the ultimate beauty treatment: it will rehydrate your skin and plump up and reduce those wrinkles, and the vitamin C-loaded berries will help clear up any spots and blemishes.

Serves 1

* 150 g/5½ oz strawberries
* 85 g/3 oz raspberries
* 85 g/3 oz blackberries
* 175 ml/6 fl oz chilled water
* small handful of ice (optional)

Berry bonus

We all know that summer berries contain vitamin C, but did you know that raspberries contain manganese, which helps with the metabolism of carbohydrates, proteins and cholesterol and helps to keep our bones healthy? Berries are also great for keeping your digestive tract in good health; their tiny fibrous seeds help keep our food moving through the body and prevent constipation.

Now for the blender...

Cut a strawberry in half and reserve one half, along with a raspberry and a blackberry. Remove the hulls from the remaining strawberries. Put the strawberries, raspberries, blackberries and water in a blender and whizz until smooth. Half-fill a glass with ice (if using), then pour in the juice. Thread the fruit onto a wooden skewer to make a stirrer, then serve with the juice.

Fab frozen berries!
Keep a supply of berries in the freezer. Let
them defrost slightly or partly thaw in the
microwave before blitzing them into a juice.

Lychee & pineapple pep-up

Create a drink with a taste of South East Asia, using fragrant lemon grass and lychees blended with pineapple and melon.

Serves 1

* 1½ lemon grass stems
* 4 tbsp boiling water
* 6 lychees, peeled and pitted
* ½ small pineapple, peeled and cut into thick slices
* ¼ honeydew melon, thickly sliced and peel removed
* small handful of ice (optional)

To make this juice

Cut the whole lemon grass stem in half lengthways, then crossways. Bruise it with a rolling pin to release its flavour, then put it in a shallow bowl and add the boiling water. Cover and leave to go cold, then drain and reserve the soaking water. Feed the softened lemon grass, lychees and pineapple, then melon through a juicer. Mix in the reserved soaking water. Half-fill a glass with ice (if using), then pour in the juice and serve immediately with the remaining half-lemon grass stem as a stirrer.

Stay hydrated for sport

It's especially important to keep fluid levels up pre- and post-sport. Drinking a healthy juice before any physical activity may keep your heart rate and body temperature lower.

Citrus refresher

Not for the faint-hearted, this fresh, zingy smoothie will certainly wake you up if you're having a mid-morning slump.

Serves 1

* 1 pink grapefruit, zest and a little pith removed, deseeded and roughly chopped
* 1 orange, zest and a little pith removed, deseeded and roughly chopped
* ½ lemon, zest and pith removed, deseeded and roughly chopped
* ½ lime, zest and pith removed, deseeded and roughly chopped, plus 1 slice to decorate

Whizz it up

Put all the ingredients in a blender and whizz until smooth. Pour into a glass, decorate with the slice of lime and serve.

Cut down on caffeine

Most of us drink far too much caffeine-loaded tea and coffee. Rather than quenching your thirst, it can lead to dehydration and reduce your stimulus to drink. In fact caffeine drinks shouldn't even be counted as part of your daily fluid intake requirement. Once you start choosing home-made, super-healthy, rehydrating juices, you will see a difference: they not only boost fluid levels, but also super-charge the body's nutrient levels in one easy-to-digest hit.

Energy

Energy-boosting facts

If you need a quick energy boost, make your juice rich in naturally sweet fruits, such as apples, oranges and berries. For a sustained boost, choose fruits and vegetables with less sugar and more starch, such as beetroots, bananas and avocados, plus ground grains and seeds.

Types of carbohydrates

Carbohydrates supply energy to the body. The digestive system converts them into glucose (blood sugar) and this is then carried in the blood and used for energy. Carbohydrates can be broken down into three groups: sugar, starches and fibre.

Sugar

Try to focus your sugar consumption on natural sugars found in fruits and vegetables rather than refined sugars found in biscuits, cakes, pastries, jams, soft drinks, sweets and some ready-prepared foods.

Starches

Good sources of starch include bananas, parsnips, sweet potatoes, carrots, beetroots, sweetcorn and wholegrain cereals. Refined starches (the baddies) are found in biscuits, pastries, cakes, sugary breakfast cereals, white bread, pasta and rice, among other foods.

Fibre

Fibre is found in fruits and vegetables, cereals (especially wholegrains), pulses, nuts and seeds.

Sugar overload

The pancreas secretes insulin, and this controls your body's uptake of glucose (blood sugar). If your diet is too high in sugar, you can upset the delicate balance of your blood-sugar level, causing fluctuations in energy and mood that can make you feel tired and irritable. The excess sugar is then stored in the liver as glycogen and as fat around the body.

Juices after exercise

If we have too little energy we may tire quickly, lose concentration and have delayed recovery. Therefore, after exercise, it is important to boost our energy levels, and a freshly made juice is a good way to do this. The most effective refuelling occurs within 30 minutes of exercise.

What is an isotonic drink?

An isotonic drink is a sports drink used to replace fluids and electrolytes and has a similar concentration to the body's own fluids. Generally made up of glucose and water, isotonic drinks contain added vitamins and salts to compensate for those lost during sweating. Typically, they contain between four and eight per cent carbohydrates, to improve stamina. They are usually commercially made, but can be home-made with an equal mix of fresh fruit or vegetable juice and water, and a pinch of salt.

Hypertonic drinks contain between 10 and 15 per cent carbohydrates and rarely contain electrolytes. The higher the level of carbohydrates in a drink, the greater the energy boost and the slower the stomach will empty, reducing urine output and encouraging fluid retention. They should only be consumed during and after endurance events such as a marathon run, but make sure you follow up with water to rehydrate later. Choose fruit smoothies or drinks made with whole fruits or vegetables such as bananas, avocados or beetroots, and soya yogurt or milk.

Hypotonic drinks are intended to quickly replace water lost during sweating. They do not generally contain carbohydrates, but they do contain sodium and potassium, which tend to be lost when we sweat.

Water to aid concentration

Ever sat at your desk and struggled to concentrate? Then it might not just be an energy boost you need. Water and natural fruit juices are also essential. Your brain is made up of 75 per cent water, so keeping hydrated is vital. When you are dehydrated, your concentration can decrease by 13 per cent and your short-term memory by seven per cent, so keep your fluid levels up – especially when revising for an exam. We also need water to help maintain normal blood pressure and body temperature. It is important to drink plenty of fluids, even when you don't feel thirsty, especially in hot weather or after exercise. Aim for a mix of fresh juices or water rather than caffeine-loaded tea or coffee, which can dehydrate, or sugary commercial drinks.

Blueberry blast

The blueberry is a superhero in the food world. When mixed with pear, natural yogurt and thirst-quenching chilled water, as in this drink, it will get you through the most hectic of schedules. You can use two apples instead of the water if you prefer; just juice them with the pear.

Serves 1

* 1 pear, halved
* 115 g/4 oz blueberries
* 175 ml/6 fl oz cup natural yogurt
* 20 g/¾ oz wheat germ
* 175 ml/6 fl oz chilled water
* small handful of crushed ice (optional)

How to make it

Feed the pear through a juicer. Pour the juice into a blender, add the blueberries, yogurt, wheat germ and water and whizz. Add the crushed ice (if using) and whizz again, until smooth. Pour into a glass and serve immediately.

Blueberries: good mood food

The antioxidant power of blueberries has been shown to help stabilize brain function and protect the neural tissue from oxidative stress – which may improve memory and learning and reduce symptoms of depression.

Keep it for later...
*If you don't drink this all at once
the wheat germ tends to swell, so you
might need to add an extra splash of
water when you finish it later.*

Single shot sports boosters

Have one of these potent juices just before you start strenuous exercise for a vitamin and mineral boost to energize muscles and aid performance. Transport them to the gym in a well-sealed insulated sports flask.

Serves 1

Beetroot booster
* 2 beetroots, halved
* 4 tbsp chilled water (optional)

Kiwi fruit booster
* 2 kiwi fruits

Blueberry booster
* 150 g/5½ oz blueberries
* 4 tbsp chilled water

To make these juices

* For the Beetroot booster, feed the beetroot through a juicer. Pour into a glass, top up with the water (if using) and serve.

* For the Kiwi fruit booster, feed the kiwi fruits through a juicer. Pour into a glass and serve.

* For the Blueberry booster, put the blueberries and water in a blender, then whizz until smooth. Pour into a glass and serve.

Water versus juices

When you exercise you lose many of the minerals in your body through sweat. Water alone will rehydrate you, but so can juices. Home-made fruit and vegetable juices also boost your energy and vitamin and mineral intake and help you rehydrate more quickly, speeding up recovery time. But best of all is to drink a mixture of the two in a home-made isotonic sports drink.

Raspberry rejuvenator

Raspberries and bananas give the body a slowly released energy boost to re-energize you in a sustained way.

Serves 1

* 30 g/1 oz goji berries
* 1 small banana, peeled and roughly chopped
* 115 g/4 oz raspberries
* 2 oranges, juice squeezed
* small handful of crushed ice (optional)
* chilled water, to taste

Whizz it up

Put the goji berries in a blender and whizz until finely ground. Add the banana, raspberries and orange juice and whizz again. Add the crushed ice (if using) and whizz again, until smooth. Add water to taste, pour into a glass and serve immediately.

Balancing your carbs & protein

For sportsmen and sportswomen it's particularly important to get the right mix of protein and carbohydrates. Too few carbs and your low energy levels will make it difficult for you to train and perform at your best, and your body will use any protein in your food and drink for energy rather than for building muscles.

Juicing oranges

Oranges vary hugely in the amount of juice
that they produce. If they are kept at room
temperature they will be easier to squeeze.
Adjust this juice with water as needed.

Pink energy

Freshly juiced, exotically fragrant papaya, as well as strawberries and lime, make this a zingy drink. The addition of soya milk makes it easy to digest and energy-boosting.

Serves 1

* ½ papaya, peeled, deseeded and roughly chopped
* 150 g/5½ oz strawberries, hulled
* 1 banana, peeled and roughly chopped
* ½ lime, juice squeezed
* 225 ml/8 fl oz unsweetened rice, almond or soya milk
* small handful of crushed ice (optional)

Ready, steady, go...

Put the papaya, strawberries and banana in a blender and whizz. Add the lime juice and milk and whizz again. Add the crushed ice (if using) and whizz again, until smooth. Pour into a glass and serve.

Papaya for pain-relief

Papaya contains the enzyme papain, which is similar to pepsin (produced by the human digestive system to break down proteins). It also exhibits pain-relieving properties, so helps to soothe your stomach, and inflammation and muscle pain after exercise. Half a medium fruit will provide an adult's daily allowance of vitamin C and contains beta carotene and small amounts of calcium and iron.

Turbo express

This smoothie includes everything you need to revitalize your body after a strenuous training session: rehydrating melon, energy-boosting banana, vitamin C-packed grapes and iron-rich watercress – you're sorted!

Serves 1

* ¼ honeydew melon, deseeded, peeled and roughly chopped
* 1 banana, peeled and roughly chopped
* 1 kiwi fruit, peeled and roughly chopped
* 115 g/4 oz green seedless grapes
* small handful of watercress (optional)
* 125 ml/4 fl oz unsweetened rice, almond or soya milk
* small handful of crushed ice (optional)

Now blitz your juice!

Put the melon, banana, kiwi fruit, grapes and watercress (if using) in a blender and whizz. Add the milk and crushed ice (if using) and whizz again, until smooth. Pour into a glass and serve immediately.

Wow, watercress!

Watercress is packed with antioxidants, minerals and vitamins C and K. It's also rich in chlorophyll, which assists with oxygenation and the health of, and number of, blood cells, so helps to fight fatigue.

Turbo express
page 91

Pink energy
page 90

Peach
energizer

Peach energizer

The grapefruit blast in this drink will perk you up and sharpen your senses, while the peach will provide natural sugars to boost your energy levels and the ginger will soothe and comfort. It's so much better for you than a cup of tea and a chocolate biscuit!

Serves 1

* 1 pink or ruby grapefruit, zest and a little pith removed, halved
* 1 carrot, halved
* 1-cm/½-inch piece of fresh ginger
* 1 large peach, pitted and roughly chopped
* 1 tbsp light tahini
* 125 ml/4 fl oz chilled water (optional)
* small handful of crushed ice

Make it peachy

Feed the grapefruit and then carrot and ginger through a juicer. Pour the juice into a blender, add the peach, tahini, water (if using) and crushed ice and whizz until smooth. Pour into a glass and serve immediately.

Plum power

This pretty, icy fruit shake will cool you down while giving you a quick burst of energy from the plums and honey and more sustainable energy from the yogurt.

Serves 1

* 125 g/4½ oz damsons, pitted
* 100 ml/3½ fl oz water
* 2 tsp clear honey
* 2 scoops of natural frozen yogurt
* 1 Italian almond or pistachio biscotti, crumbled, to decorate (optional)
* ¼ plum, pitted, to decorate (optional)

Ice, ice baby

Put the damsons, water and honey in a small saucepan over a medium heat. Stir, cover tightly, reduce the heat to low and simmer for 15 minutes, until the damsons have split and are very soft. Leave to cool. Pour the mixture into a blender, add the frozen yogurt and whizz until smooth. Pour into a glass, sprinkle over the biscotti (if using), decorate the rim with the plum (if using) and serve immediately.

Plums for vitamin C

Plums are a great source of vitamin C, which helps you to fight infection and increase iron absorption. But don't eat too many in one go as they are known to have a laxative effect.

Boost brain power

After intense concentration or physical exercise, energy levels plummet. Not having enough glucose in the blood makes us feel weak and tired. Glucose enables good concentration and focus. However, once your blood glucose is in the normal range you cannot boost your brain power further by increasing your glucose levels.

Ginger energizer

The ginger in this oh-so-good-for-you veggie drink will pep you up when you're feeling sluggish.

Serves 1

* 2 carrots, halved
* 4 tomatoes, roughly chopped
* 1 tbsp lemon juice
* 30 g/1 oz fresh flat-leaf parsley
* 3-cm/1¼-inch piece of fresh ginger, peeled and finely grated
* small handful of crushed ice
* 125 ml/4 fl oz chilled water

To make this juice

Feed the carrots through a juicer. Pour the juice into a blender, add the tomatoes and lemon juice and whizz. Add the parsley (reserving a stem to decorate), ginger and crushed ice and whizz again, until smooth. Add the water and whizz again. Pour into a glass, garnish with the parsley stem and serve immediately.

Good-for-you ginger

Ginger has been used as a natural remedy for centuries, especially for ailments involving the digestive system. Pregnant women are often encouraged to drink ginger tea to prevent morning sickness. Recent studies have shown that ginger may also help with menstrual cramps, migraines, colds, flu and heartburn.

Power gulp

Beetroot is the favourite vegetable among sportsmen and sportswomen. It's great for boosting stamina and making muscles work harder, and packed with vitamins, minerals, carbohydrates, protein and powerful antioxidants. All that's missing is fat, and that's no bad thing!

Serves 1

* 2 beetroots, halved
* 30 g/1 oz flaxseeds (linseeds)
* 4 plums, quartered and pitted
* 150 g/5½ oz seedless red grapes
* 225 ml/8 fl oz chilled water
* ice, to serve (optional)

Give it a whirl

Feed the beetroots through a juicer. Put the flaxseeds in a blender and whizz until finely ground. Add the beetroot juice, plums, grapes and water and whizz until smooth. Pour into a glass, add ice (if using) and serve immediately.

Blending bananas

Bananas, like apples, discolour, so
make sure you serve this juice
straight from the blender.

Apple attack

This juice provides a good combination of natural sugars for instant energy and soluble fibre for slow-release energy, and is a great source of protein and calcium for building strong muscles and bones.

Serves 1

* 2 apples, halved
* 1 small banana, peeled and roughly chopped
* 2 tbsp natural yogurt
* 1 tbsp light tahini
* ½ tsp sesame seeds, to decorate

How to make it

Feed the apples through a juicer. Pour the juice into a blender, add the banana, yogurt and tahini and whizz again, until smooth. Pour into a glass, sprinkle with sesame seeds and serve.

Apples for energy

Apples give a great energy-boosting natural fruit sugar hit. They also contain pectin (the setting agent in jam), vitamins and minerals. Pectin helps to remove excess cholesterol and toxic metals from the digestive tract and stimulates friendly bacteria in the large intestine. Perhaps that's why our mothers and grannies used to say 'an apple a day keeps the doctor away'.

Muscular magic

It would be easy to believe that just looking at this green drink could make you feel healthier! The good news is that it really is bursting with vitamins and minerals.

Serves 1

* 55 g/2 oz green curly kale
* small handful of fresh flat-leaf parsley
* ½ romaine lettuce
* 2 celery sticks, halved
* 1 apple, halved
* ½ lemon
* 30 g/1 oz flaked almonds
* ½ avocado, pitted and flesh scooped from the skin
* small handful of crushed ice

To make this juice

Feed the kale, then the parsley and lettuce, then the celery, apple and lemon through a juicer. Put the almonds in a blender and whizz until finely ground. Add the kale juice mix and avocado flesh and whizz again, until smooth. Add the crushed ice and whizz again. Pour into a glass and serve immediately.

Post-exercise boost

Nutritionists recommend that after exercise you have a healthy snack within 30 minutes to help promote muscle repair and growth.

Natural apple booster

Feeling stressed and tired? Then enjoy this comforting apple-pie-in-a-glass with a hint of honey and cinnamon. You could try organic brown rice syrup instead of honey for a lighter, nuttier flavour.

Serves 1

* 3 apples, halved
* 2 tsp flax oil
* 1 tsp clear honey
* pinch of ground cinnamon
* small handful of crushed ice (optional)
* 1 cinnamon stick (optional)

Mix it up

Feed the apples through a juicer. Stir in the flax oil, honey and ground cinnamon. Pour the juice into a blender, add the crushed ice (if using) and whizz. Pour into a glass and serve with the cinnamon stick as a stirrer (if using).

Juicing apples

Apple juice discolours quickly, so make this juice just before you need it. The colour of the juice will depend on the colour of the apple skins; for a juice with a hint of pink, use red-skinned apples.

Muscular magic

page 102

Natural apple
booster

page 103

Tropical refresher

Papaya and mango are both rich in natural fruit sugars, which give an energy boost. They're easy to digest and gentle on the stomach.

Serves 1

* 1 banana, peeled and roughly chopped
* ½ papaya, peeled, deseeded and roughly chopped
* ½ mango, pitted, peeled and roughly chopped
* 1 lime, juice squeezed
* 2-cm/¾-inch piece of fresh ginger, peeled and finely grated
* 2 tsp hemp oil
* 125 ml/4 fl oz unsweetened rice, almond or soya milk
* small handful of crushed ice

For a tropical island dream...

Put the banana, papaya and mango in a blender and whizz until smooth. Add the lime, ginger, hemp oil, milk and crushed ice and whizz again. Pour into a glass and serve immediately.

Superfood: kale

From shiny blue-green to red, this ruffled, leafy vegetable boasts a healthy amount of calcium, vitamin B, vitamin C and beta carotene. The antioxidant lutein helps to protect us from macular eye degeneration, while indoles offer protection against oestrogen-related cancers and sulforaphane may help boost the liver's ability to detoxify carcinogenic compounds. Back in 1939, the government encouraged everyone to grow kale in the 'Dig for Victory' campaign as it is easy for even a novice gardener to grow and highly nutritious.

Cranberry & pineapple fatigue-buster

This fruit combination works really well, with the natural sweetness of the pineapple balancing the sharpness of the cranberries. It can be made in advance and taken to a training session in a flask to give an energizing boost to valuable glycogen stores pre- and post-exercise.

Serves 1

* 30 g/1 oz chia seeds
* ½ small pineapple, peeled and roughly chopped
* 115 g/4 oz cranberries
* small handful of ice (if using)

Give it a whirl

Put the chia seeds in a blender and whizz until finely ground. Add the pineapple and cranberries and whizz again, until smooth. Half-fill a glass with ice (if using), pour in the juice and serve immediately.

Tummy soothing pineapple

Rich in energy-boosting fruit sugars and vitamin C, pineapple also contains the digestive enzyme bromelain, which can have a calming effect on the stomach and so help anyone who feels nauseous after a strenuous workout or marathon run. It is also thought to act as an anti-inflammatory agent to accelerate tissue repair, and so may help to aid the recovery of bruising, blisters and sprains.

Preparing pineapples

Juicers have different sized motors. Those with a smaller motor may not be able to cope with pineapple skin, which is why it is cut off in this book. Check your manual and see if you need to cut the skin off before juicing.

Green energy

This super-smoothie is packed with antioxidants, vitamins and minerals. The spirulina is a great protein-booster too.

Serves 1

* 1 pear, halved
* 40 g/1½ oz young spinach
* 4 stems of fresh flat-leaf parsley
* ¼ cucumber, roughly chopped
* ½ avocado, pitted and flesh scooped from the skin
* ½ tsp spirulina powder
* chilled water, to taste
* 1 brazil nut, roughly chopped

Mix it up

Feed the pear through a juicer. Pour the juice into a blender, add the spinach, parsley, cucumber and avocado and whizz until smooth. Pour into a glass. Mix the spirulina with just enough water to make a thick liquid, then swirl this into the juice. Sprinkle over the chopped brazil nut, then serve.

Ripening avocados

Just-ripe avocados will have the best flavour. f you have one that is slightly under-ripe, put it in a brown paper bag and store it in a warm place such as on a sunny windowsill or in the airing cupboard to help it ripen.

Avocado benefits

Avocados may inhibit the growth of prostate cancer and, being high in oleic acid, they may also help to prevent breast cancer. They contain more of the carotenoid lutein than any other commonly consumed fruit. Lutein protects against macular degeneration and cataracts, two disabling age-related eye diseases. Eating avocados may also lower your cholesterol levels and, as an excellent source of glutathione, they even contain anti-ageing properties.

Mango & lime bone-builder

This pretty, green-speckled drink looks mango-free, but the fruit's natural sweetness balances the kale, and its flavour comes through even if its colour is disguised.

Serves 1

* 1 tbsp sesame seeds
* ½ lime, juice squeezed
* 30 g/1 oz green curly kale, torn into pieces
* 1 mango, pitted, peeled and roughly chopped
* 225 ml/8 fl oz unsweetened rice, almond or soya milk
* small handful of crushed ice

Give it a whirl

Put the sesame seeds in a blender and whizz until finely ground. Add the lime juice, kale and mango and whizz until blended. Add the milk and crushed ice and whizz again, until smooth. Pour into a glass and serve immediately.

Good for your bones

Calcium-boosting sesame seeds, kale and fortified soya milk all help to maintain bone strength and function of the nerves and muscles. The addition of vitamin D to the soya milk aids absorption.

Grape & lychee reviver

Go oriental with fragrant lychees, thought by the Chinese to be the symbol of love. Blend them with creamy, smooth avocado and naturally sweet grapes for the perfect pick-me-up to rehydrate and fight fatigue.

Serves 1

* 300 g/10½ oz green grapes
* 55 g/2 oz young spinach
* ½ ripe avocado, pitted and flesh scooped from the skin, plus a slice to serve (optional)
* 5 lychees, peeled and pitted
* small handful of crushed ice
* 125 ml/4 fl oz chilled water

Whizz it up

Feed the grapes and spinach through a juicer. Pour the juice into a blender, add the avocado, lychees and crushed ice and whizz until smooth. Add the water and whizz again. Pour into a glass, add the avocado slice (if using) and serve immediately.

Grape nutrition

Grapes are a good source of potassium, although weight for weight they provide only one-twentieth of the vitamin C of kiwi fruits. The Greeks regarded them as an aphrodisiac, as they are the fruit of Dionysus, the Greek god of fertility and procreation.

Super-powered mango

You don't need to be a sportsman or sportswoman to benefit from an energy boost; coping with a young family can be just as tiring! Rather than reach for a chocolate biscuit or slice of cake to pick you up in the middle of the afternoon, try this energizing fruit blend of clementines, mango and apples. If clementines are out of season, you can use an orange.

Serves 1

* 2 clementines, zest and a little pith removed
* 1 mango, pitted and peeled
* 2 apples, halved
* small handful of ice, to serve (optional)
* chilled water, to taste
* 1 tsp clear honey

How to make this juice

Feed the clementines, mango and apples through a juicer. Half-fill a glass with ice (if using). Pour in the juice, top up with water to taste, stir in the honey and serve immediately.

How to prepare mango

Cut a thick slice off the top of the mango using a sharp knife, then cut one off the bottom to reveal a large, flattish oval stone. Cut around the stone, keeping all the trimmings. Push out the skin, cut the flesh into cubes, then cut the cubes off the skin.

Mango for energy

A mango is 14 per cent natural sugar, and this can be quickly converted into energy by the body. It is also rich in beta carotene and vitamin C.

Health

Fruit & veg nutrition

Your weight, energy levels, complexion and mood are all influenced by the foods you eat. Making smart dietary choices can help to protect and restore your health. Here's a guide to the nutrition of fruit and vegetables.

Apples, pears & plums

These orchard fruits are good sources of vitamin C, soluble pectin (which is thought to help lower cholesterol) and the minerals calcium, magnesium and phosphorus.

Tropical fruits

When it comes to mango, papaya, melon and pineapple, the more highly coloured the fruit, the more healthy carotenoids it will contain, including beta carotene. These fruits are also rich in vitamin C.

Berries

Strawberries, raspberries, blackberries and blueberries are good sources of vitamin C and fibre. The different fruits contain varying amounts of vitamin A, B vitamins and minerals and have antiviral and antibacteria properties. Good antioxidants may help to lower cholesterol.

Bananas

Bananas are rich in complex carbohydrates to boost energy, potassium to regulate blood pressure, and tryptophan and vitamin B6 to boost serotonin (the good-mood chemical).

What counts as a portion?

Health professionals recommend that you eat at least five portions of fresh fruit and vegetables each day. One 150 ml/5 fl oz or more glass of fruit or vegetable juice made in a juicer counts as one of your five-a-day. But even if you drink several glasses they will still only count as one portion. However, two 150 ml/5 fl oz glasses of fruit smoothie (as opposed to juices) can count as two of your five a day, as they are blended rather than juiced and so often contain the whole fruit, which means more fibre, antioxidants and other nutrients should be present. But if you drink more than two smoothies per day they will still only count as two of your five a day.

Broccoli & kale

Kale and broccoli are two of the most well-known superfoods, rich in antioxidants, vitamins C and K, calcium, magnesium and zinc.

Green leafy vegetables

Spinach, Swiss chard, romaine lettuce and watercress are rich in vitamin B complex, needed to make serotonin (a mood-boosting chemical). They are also loaded with antioxidants to help reduce the risk of heart disease and cancer. They contain lutein, a carotenoid antioxidant that helps protect against cataracts and macular degeneration, and a good mix of minerals.

Root veg

Root vegetables such as beetroots, carrots, sweet potatoes and parsnips are the storage organs of the plants they support. They are packed with fibre, starch and sugar, so are good for boosting energy. They also contain vitamins and minerals, antioxidants and phytonutrients.

Onions, leeks & garlic

Sulphur compounds found in onions, leeks and garlic help us to relax and enlarge blood vessels to reduce blood pressure. Allicin in garlic and onions is antibacterial and antiviral and may help us fight colds, flu, stomach viruses and candida yeast. They can also help reduce inflammation, so may relieve arthritis and protect against asthma attacks.

Avocados

Avocados contain more protein than any other fruit. They also contain antioxidant vitamins and are super-high in vitamin C and potassium. They do contain healthy monosaturated fats, which makes their calorie count higher than that of any other fruit.

Antioxidants explained

Lots of fruit and vegetables contain antioxidants. These may be an important part of the diet and involved in DNA and cell maintenance and repair. Vitamins C and E are antioxidants, as are the minerals zinc and selenium. It is thought antioxidants may help reduce the production of free radicals, preventing early damage to cells and potentially reducing incidence of cancer, heart disease and brain-function decline.

A helping hand

While it's great to make a juice with a mixture of different fruits and vegetables, sometimes you just don't have the time or the ingredients in the fridge. These three quick juices all consist of just one ingredient plus a supplement to boost their nutrient values.

1

Apple & spirulina

* 2 apples, halved
* 1 tsp spirulina powder

Spirulina

This dark green algae has 10 times more calcium than milk, and 58 times more iron than spinach. It contains 60 per cent protein, and is rich in essential fatty acids and vitamin B12. (Also see page 70.)

Serves 1

For each of these drinks, feed the fruit or vegetable through a juicer, then pour the juice into a jam jar. Add the powder, screw on the lid and shake really well, so that the finished drink doesn't taste powdery. Pour into a glass and serve immediately.

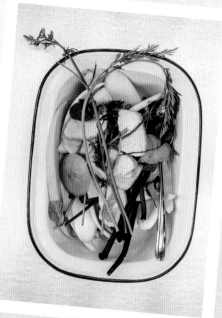

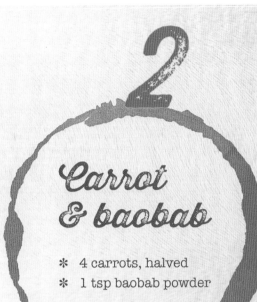

2

Carrot
& baobab

* 4 carrots, halved
* 1 tsp baobab powder

Pears for immunity

Pears contain antioxidants, including vitamin C and copper. Antioxidants encourage a strong immune system and help our bodies to fight off disease and illness.

3

Pear &
wheatgrass

* 2 pears, halved
* 1 tsp wheatgrass powder

Baobab

Baobab is an African fruit that has six times more potassium than bananas, six times more vitamin C than oranges, six times more antioxidants than blueberries, twice as many antioxidants as goji berries and twice as much calcium as milk.

Ripe pears

Don't worry if the pears are a little hard; you will still be able to extract masses of juice.

Wheatgrass

Wheatgrass contains all 8 essential amino acids. It also contains vitamins E, K and B complex (especially B12) and chlorophyll and is rich in calcium, vitamin C and iron. Freshly juiced wheatgrass is the best for you, but wheatgrass powder makes a quick, convenient alternative and is a great storecupboard standby.

Cranberry soother

Help to protect your body with this wonderfully colourful and tasty drink. It's a great way to encourage your children to eat more vitamin-C-packed fruit, too.

Serves 1

* 150 g/5½ oz cranberries
* 1 orange, juice squeezed
* 5 tbsp natural yogurt
* 2 tsp clear honey

Cool cranberries

Cranberries contain significant amounts of antioxidants and other phytonutrients that may help protect against heart disease and cancer. As well as helping to prevent infections of the urinary tract, they are thought to be beneficial to the health of your heart and teeth. They may also help prevent ulcers and are thought to have anti-ageing properties.

Whizz it up

Put the cranberries and orange juice in a blender and whizz until smooth. Add the yogurt and honey and whizz again. Pour into a glass and serve.

Up the anti

Protect your body from the inside out with this fresh, fruity drink that is bursting with antioxidants, the body's defence team.

Serves 1

* ½ avocado, pitted and flesh scooped from the skin
* 115 g/4 oz blueberries
* 115 g/4 oz strawberries, hulled
* 1 tangerine or small orange, juice squeezed
* 125 ml/4 fl oz chilled water
* small handful of crushed ice (optional)

To make this juice

Put the avocado, blueberries, strawberries, tangerine juice and water in a blender and whizz. Add the crushed ice (if using) and whizz again, until smooth. Pour into a glass and serve.

Soothing smoothie

Cranberries are soothing for the digestive and urinary tracts. They are also a good source of cancer-fighting phytochemicals. This juice is packed with vitamin C, plus potassium for regulating blood pressure.

Serves 1

* 1 orange
* 55 g/2 oz cranberries
* 1 banana, peeled and roughly chopped
* 100 ml/3½ fl oz soya yogurt

Go bananas!

Cut the zest from the orange and finely shred and reserve a little of it; discard the rest. Remove the pips and most of the pith and discard them. Roughly chop the flesh and put it and the cranberries in a blender, then whizz. Add the banana and yogurt and whizz again, until smooth. Pour into a glass, sprinkle with the shredded orange zest and serve.

Sweet banana

Once bananas have brown speckles on the skin, they become naturally sweeter and easier to digest. When combined with protein-rich soya yogurt as in this drink, they provide a more sustaining, longer-lasting energy fix.

Stress buster

Ginseng is a natural stimulant that helps to combat stress and lifts the mood. This teatime juice also aids liver and kidney function and prevents fluid retention.

Serves 1

* 1 ginseng tea bag or 1 tsp ginseng tea
* 150 ml/5 fl oz boiling water
* 1 apple, halved
* 40 g/1½ oz rocket leaves

Time for tea

Put the tea bag in a cup, pour over the boiling water and leave to stand for 4 minutes. Strain the water into a glass. Feed the apple and then rocket through a juicer. Stir the juice into the tea and serve warm or cold.

Looking after your skin

Give yourself a facial from the inside out with this drink. Every skin pore eliminates waste and sweat and the sebaceous glands help to remove toxins. The skin reflects what is happening inside our bodies; if we are stressed, run-down or have overdone things a little, our skin will look tired and lifeless, with spots and blemishes.

The glory of ginseng

Ginseng is a slow-growing plant with fleshy roots. It typically grows in northern China, Korea and eastern Siberia. As well as being believed to be a powerful aphrodisiac and tonic, it may also act as an appetite-suppressant, which can help to encourage weight loss. Ginseng tea is additionally believed to be effective against menstrual stomach pain.

Parsley purifier

As a diuretic, this drink really helps to purify your body. The strong flavours of the herbs and spinach are balanced by the natural sweetness of the sugar snap peas and the deliciously delicate flavour of the cucumber.

Serves 1

* 115 g/4 oz sugar snap peas
* small handful of fresh flat-leaf parsley
* 2 stems of fresh rosemary
* 1 garlic clove
* 55 g/2 oz young spinach
* ½ cucumber
* 2 celery sticks, halved
* 1 tsp hemp oil
* chilled water, to taste
* ice, to serve (optional)

Give it a whirl

Feed the sugar snap peas, parsley (reserving 1 stem to garnish), rosemary and garlic, then spinach, then cucumber and celery through a juicer. Pour into a glass, stir in the hemp oil and water to taste, garnish with the parsley stem and serve with ice (if using).

Take a fresh look at celery, parsley & rosemary

Celery has been used as a diuretic for centuries and helps to flush excess fluid from the body. It also contains phthalides, which have been shown to lower blood pressure by relaxing muscles around the arteries, allowing blood vessels to dilute. Celery contains calcium, magnesium and potassium, which help regulate blood pressure. Parsley is rich in calcium and potassium too, and has lots of iron, phosphorus and sodium. Just 2 tablespoons of parsley contain a whopping 153 per cent of the recommended daily allowance of vitamin K (which works with protein to help strengthen bones, and helps prevent build-up of calcium in the tissues that can lead to atherosclerosis, cardiovascular disease and stroke). Used by herbalists for centuries, rosemary also acts as a diuretic. It is anti-inflammatory and antiseptic too, and can help to calm digestive pains.

Ginger pep-up

Pretty and fragrant, with the warmth of ginger, this juice will brighten a less-than-perfect summer's day.

Serves 1

* 2 pears, halved
* 4 oranges, juice squeezed
* 4 cubes of crystallized ginger

Spice things up

Feed the pears through a juicer. Pour the juice into a blender, add the orange juice and crystallized ginger and whizz until smooth. Pour into a glass and serve.

Pears for health

Fresh pear juice, rich in natural fruit sugars, takes the edge off the sharpness of citrus juice. Pears have a high water content, and their pectin helps to lower cholesterol and acts as a diuretic and mild laxative. They also contain flavanoids. Cloudy pear juice contains 40 per cent more phenolic phytonutrients and more antioxidants than filtered.

Tummy soother

Pineapple juice is great for improving digestion and soothing an upset tummy. The healing enzyme bromelain reduces bruising, so it can help with recovery from an injury. It's also a good source of vitamin C, which helps to heal and fight infection.

Serves 1

* ½ sweet pineapple, peeled and cut into thick slices, plus a leaf to decorate
* 1 lemon, zest and most of the pith removed, halved
* 2-cm/¾-inch piece of fresh ginger

Ready, steady, go!

Feed the pineapple, lemon and ginger through a juicer. Pour into a glass, add a pineapple leaf as a stirrer if you wish and serve. Remove the pineapple leaf before drinking.

Green goddess

This cooling, cleansing drink is good for liver and kidney function, helps lower cholesterol and relieves tension and insomnia. It's high in iron and chlorophyll, which benefits your eyes and helps maintain healthy blood vessels.

Serves 1

* ½ Galia melon, thickly sliced and peel removed
* 85 g/3 oz young spinach
* 2 large stems of fresh flat-leaf parsley
* 3 large stems of fresh mint
* small handful of ice (optional)

Time to juice

Feed the melon, then spinach, parsley and 2 stems of mint through a juicer. Half-fill a glass with ice (if using), then pour in the juice, garnish with the remaining stem of mint and serve immediately.

Crimson vitality

Good health depends on every cell in the body receiving its fair share of nutrition. Your blood absorbs vital nutrition and circulates round the body. What better or easier way for the body to digest vital vitamins and minerals than through this vitality-boosting beetroot juice?

Serves 1

* 1 beetroot, halved
* 115 g/4 oz cranberries
* 1-cm/½-inch piece of fresh ginger
* 2 apples, halved
* small handful of ice (optional)
* chilled water, to taste

In the pink...

Feed the beetroot, then cranberries and ginger, then apples through a juicer. Half-fill a glass with ice (if using), pour in the juice, top up with water to taste and serve immediately.

Use the beetroot leaves!

If your beetroot has fresh, vibrant leaves rather than tired, limp-looking ones, add them to the juicer too.

Superfood: beetroots

Beetroot is packed with minerals, vitamins, carbohydrates, protein, fibre and antioxidants. When betacyanin, the pigment that gives beetroot its colour, combines with carotenoids and flavonoids and is consumed regularly, it is believed that it may help reduce the oxidation of LDL cholesterol. This in turn protects artery walls and reduces the risk of heart disease and strokes. Recent research has found that regular intake of beetroot juice helps to lower high blood pressure. Beetroot is also rich in potassium and folic acid and contains iron, so is good for those with anaemia or fatigue. The high levels of nitrites have been shown to benefit sportsmen and sportswomen, and may even help to slow the progression of dementia.

Spring clean

This dark-coloured juice tastes surprisingly light and fresh. The wheatgrass has long been associated with healing properties.

Serves 1

* 115 g/4 oz broccoli, broken into large florets
* 2 apples, halved
* 1 courgette, halved
* 1 tsp wheatgrass powder
* small handful of ice

To make this juice

Feed the broccoli, then apples and courgette through a juicer. Add the wheatgrass powder and whisk until smooth. Half-fill a glass with ice, pour in the juice and serve immediately.

Wonderful wheatgrass

Modern medics have mixed views on the health benefits of wheatgrass. Yes, it is rich in chlorophyll and protein and contains vitamins A, C, E, K and B12 plus a range of minerals, but nothing else is certain. Some homeopaths believe that it may help reduce the side-effects of chemotherapy. It is sold in trays in health-food shops.

Body balancer

Look quickly at this drink and you could mistake it for a coffee swirled with hot milk, but it is actually dairy-free and caffeine-free. The prunes make it a natural laxative.

Serves 1

* 1 tbsp flaxseeds (linseeds)
* 85 g/3 oz ready-to-eat pitted prunes
* 1 small banana, peeled and roughly chopped
* 1 tbsp wheat germ
* 2 large oranges, juice squeezed
* 115 ml/4 fl oz vanilla soya yogurt
* 225 ml/8 fl oz chilled water

Whizz it up

Put the flaxseeds in a blender and whizz until finely ground. Add the prunes, banana and wheat germ and whizz again. Add the orange juice and half the yogurt and whizz again, until smooth. Add the water and whizz once more. Pour into a glass, add the remaining yogurt and swirl together with a teaspoon, then serve.

A natural laxative

Prunes are one of the most effective laxatives. They are rich in potassium, which is needed for the healthy function of cells, nerves and muscles and to regulate blood pressure. The natural cultures in the yogurt in this drink help restore the balance of healthy bacteria in your gut.

Spring clean
page 144

Body balancer
page 145

Multi-mineral bonanza

With spinach, beetroot, oranges and carrots, this drink provides a bumper beta carotene and vitamin C hit.

Serves 1

* 2 beetroots, halved
* 40 g/1½ oz young spinach
* 2 carrots, halved
* 2 oranges, zest and a little pith removed, halved
* 1 tbsp sesame seeds, finely ground
* small handful of ice
* sparkling mineral water, chilled, to taste

Mix it up!

Feed the beetroot, spinach and carrots, then oranges through a juicer. Stir in the ground sesame seeds. Half-fill a glass with ice, then pour in the juice, top up with sparkling water to taste and serve immediately.

Red pepper reviver

This fiery juice is sure to wake you up if you're having a mid-morning snooze!

Serves 1

* 2 carrots, halved, plus strips of shredded carrot to garnish
* 2 tomatoes, halved
* 1 large red pepper, halved
* 2 tsp lemon juice
* freshly ground black pepper

Ready, steady, go

Feed the carrots, then tomatoes and red pepper through a juicer. Stir in the lemon juice and plenty of black pepper. Pour into a glass, garnish with the strips of shredded carrot and serve.

Thumbs up for tomatoes

Tomatoes are rich in lycopene, a carotenoid pigment that turns them red. It is thought this may help prevent some forms of cancer. They are also a good source of potassium, with smaller amounts of vitamins C and E. They contain 90 per cent water, so are great for rehydration too.

Cutting calories

The more you get into juicing, the less appealing that takeaway snack will be. Just cutting down 100 or 200 calories a day can have a big impact on your weight over the course of a year.

Red pep-up

Full of disease-fighting, anti-ageing antioxidants, this drink provides lots of energy from its natural sweetness to help you get through the day.

Serves 1

* 2 fennel bulbs with leaves, halved
* 1 apple, halved
* 1 small red pepper, halved
* 1 carrot, halved

Give it a whirl

Remove a few leaves from the fennel and reserve. Feed the apple, then fennel and pepper, then carrot through a juicer. Pour into a glass, garnish with the fennel leaves and serve.

Winter pick-me-up

Banish the winter blues with this nutrient-packed juice that boosts vitamin, mineral and energy levels.

Serves 1

* 1 parsnip, halved
* 2 carrots, halved, plus 2 carrot sticks to garnish
* 1 garlic clove
* 2 apples, halved
* 2 tbsp porridge oats
* 1 tbsp wheat germ
* 2 tsp clear honey
* small handful of ice (optional)

Whizz it up

Feed the parsnip, carrots and garlic, then apples through a juicer. Put the oats and wheat germ in a blender and whizz until finely ground. Add the honey and parsnip juice mix and whizz again, until smooth. Half-fill a glass with ice (if using). Pour in the juice, add the carrot sticks and serve immediately.

How to use wheat germ

Wheat germ flakes swell in your drinks. This means that if you don't serve a juice or smoothie as soon as you have made it, you will need to add a splash of chilled water to return it to the right consistency.

Buying parsnips

Buy parsnips a few weeks after the first frost if you can, as much of the starch is converted to sugar in a frost, so making them taste sweeter.

Detox

Beet aid detox

This thirst-quenching, nutrient-packed juice is bursting with vitamins and minerals. Since Roman times, beetroot has been thought of as an aphrodisiac, so who knows what might happen when you feel detoxed and re-energized?

Serves 1

* 1 beetroot, halved
* ½ lime
* 55 g/2 oz red chard
* 675 g/1 lb 8 oz watermelon, thickly sliced and peel removed
* small handful of ice (optional)

Smoothie steps

Feed the beetroot and lime, then chard and watermelon through a juicer. Half-fill a glass with ice (if using), then pour in the juice and serve immediately.

Health notes

Beetroot contains virtually all the vitamins and minerals needed to give your whole body a boost. Watermelon's high water content helps to rehydrate and plump up your skin.

Citrus cleanser

Citrus fruits stimulate the digestive system. In traditional folk medicine it was thought they also acted as a cleanser and astringent, stimulating the liver and gall bladder.

Serves 1

* 1 pink or ruby grapefruit, zest and a little pith removed, halved
* 1 orange, zest and a little pith removed, halved
* 1 lime, zest and pith removed from half
* 1 large pear, halved
* small handful of ice (optional)

To make this juice

Feed the grapefruit, orange and lime, then pear through a juicer. Half-fill a glass with ice (if using), pour in the juice and serve immediately.

Pears to add sweetness

Grapefruit and lime juices can be a little sharp for some tastes, even when mixed with orange juice. Fresh pear juice, which is rich in natural fruit sugars, takes the edge off the sharpness. High in water, pear helps to rehydrate the body. The pectin in pears helps to lower cholesterol and acts as a diuretic and mild laxative.

Grapefruit nutrition

Grapefruit is a great source of vitamin C. It is packed with flavonoids (natural chemical compounds that may reduce early damage to DNA and cell membranes).

Cucumber spring clean

Think of this as a chilled gingered gazpacho, and you can enjoy the detox qualities of ginger and onion for a light lunch. If you drink it outside in the sunshine you could almost feel transported to a Mediterranean terrace.

Serves 1

* ½ romaine lettuce
* 2 tomatoes
* 2-cm/¾-inch piece of fresh ginger
* 1 spring onion
* 1 celery stick, halved
* 1 carrot, halved
* ¼ cucumber, plus a slice to garnish (optional)
* small handful of ice (optional)

Whizz it up

Feed the lettuce and tomatoes, then ginger, onion, celery, carrot and cucumber through a juicer. Half-fill a glass with ice (if using), pour in the juice, add the cucumber slice to garnish (if using) and serve immediately.

Love your lettuce

Lettuces contain the latex-like compound lactucarium, which is thought to calm and soothe the nerves and aid sleep. They are about 90 per cent water. The outer leaves supply the most beta carotene, vitamin C, folate and iron.

Know your onions

Onions, leeks and garlic are rich in antiviral and antibacterial nutrients that are thought to cleanse the system. They are most potent when eaten raw, but use just a little as they have a strong flavour.

Lettuce choice
If you don't have a romaine lettuce, choose from cos or iceberg. Little gem would also work, but you would need to use two of them.

Green jump-start

If you like spinach or watercress soup, you will love this juice. You don't
get a huge amount of juice from these green leaves, but what you
do get is concentrated with antioxidants, minerals and vitamins.
Mix them with thirst-quenching courgettes and apples for a health
boost that will jump-start your detox.

Serves 1

* 55 g/2 oz young spinach
* 30 g/1 oz watercress
* 1 courgette, halved
* 2 apples, halved
* 1 tsp wheatgrass powder
  (optional)
* small handful of ice (optional)

Give it a whirl

Feed the spinach and watercress, then
courgette and apples through a juicer.
Stir in the wheatgrass powder (if using).
Half-fill a glass with ice (if using), pour
in the juice and serve immediately.

Get into good habits

A detox can help you review your eating
habits. Most of us don't eat enough green veg,
and this tasty juice is a way to increase your
consumption easily.

Broccoli & parsley revitalizer

Wonderfully soothing and gentle, this delicate, revitalizing green juice is naturally sweet and refreshing, and makes a perfect alternative to a caffeine-loaded tea or coffee mid-afternoon.

Serves 1

* 115 g/4 oz broccoli, broken into large florets
* small handful of fresh flat-leaf parsley
* ½ fennel bulb
* 2 apples, halved
* chilled water, to taste
* small handful of ice (optional)

Fire up your juicer

Feed the broccoli and parsley, then fennel and apples through a juicer. Top up with water to taste. Half-fill a glass with ice (if using), pour in the juice and serve immediately.

Fabulous fennel

Fennel acts as a diuretic and has a calming effect on the stomach while providing useful amounts of beta carotene and folate. Parsley is also a diuretic and herbalists have long believed it helps reduce inflammation in the kidneys and bladder.

Papaya & apricot soother

Papaya and apricots blend to a wonderfully silky, smooth texture that feels soothing, especially if you are battling a sore throat. This smoothie is packed with vitamin C to help fight off the symptoms of colds and flu.

Serves 1

* ½ papaya, peeled, deseeded and roughly chopped
* 4 apricots, halved and pitted
* 2 oranges, juice squeezed
* 1 lime, juice squeezed
* small handful of crushed ice (optional)
* 4 tbsp chilled water

Mix it up

Put the papaya, apricots and orange and lime juices in a blender and whizz until smooth. Add the crushed ice (if using) and water and whizz again. Pour into a glass and serve immediately.

Best drinks for the morning

Serious fans of detoxing diets recommend that you drink fruit juices in the morning, as they believe these have a stronger detoxifying effect than vegetable juices. Fruit juices do have a mild laxative effect – and as the papaya and apricots are blended rather than juiced in this drink, it also contains soluble fibre that will help keep your digestive system moving and expel cholesterol from your body.

Broccoli & parsley revitalizer
page 164

Papaya & apricot soother
page 165

Red cabbage digestive aid

You will be amazed at the vibrant purple juice that comes from a red cabbage. While this drink might look a little like a witch's brew, it is far from wicked. It is light and aromatic, with a hint of cardamom (said to calm digestion) and the delicate sweetness of red grapes.

Serves 1

* 150 g/5¼ oz red grapes
* ½ fennel bulb
* ¼ red cabbage, roughly chopped
* 3 cardamom pods
* chilled water, to taste
* small handful of ice (optional)

Time to get started

Feed the grapes, then fennel, then red cabbage through a juicer. Roughly crush the cardamom using a pestle in a mortar, discard the pods and then finely crush the black seeds and stir them into the juice. Top up with water to taste. Half-fill a glass with ice (if using), pour in the juice and serve immediately.

Big apple detox

With its creamy, delicate flavour and cleansing ginger, this juice is perfect for after an indulgent holiday or Christmas.

Serves 1

* 1 parsnip, halved
* 5-mm/¼-inch piece of fresh ginger
* 2 apples, halved
* 125 ml/4 fl oz chilled water
* small handful of ice (optional)

Give it a whirl

Feed the parsnip and ginger, then apples through a juicer. Top up with the water. Half-fill a glass with ice (if using), pour in the juice and serve immediately.

Fresh is best

Instead of buying commercially made detox compounds or potions, freshly juice fruit and vegetables at home. Look at what you eat and when; you might find that making small changes will have a big impact. Ditch that high-calorie, full-fat coffee latte or cola and have a low-calorie, high-vitamin and high-mineral juice instead.

Nature's remedy

This drink tastes surprisingly mild, with a natural sweetness from the parsnip and carrots, and boy-oh-boy does it do you good!

Serves 1

* 2 carrots, halved
* ½ small onion
* 1 garlic clove
* 1 parsnip, halved
* 1 orange, zest and a little pith removed, halved
* 125 ml/4 fl oz chilled water
* pinch of ground turmeric
* pinch of freshly ground black pepper
* small handful of ice (optional)

Ready, steady, go

Cut a thin slice from a carrot and reserve. Feed the remaining carrots and the onion, garlic, parsnip and then orange through a juicer. Stir in the water, turmeric and pepper. Half-fill a glass with ice (if using), pour in the juice, garnish with the carrot slice and serve.

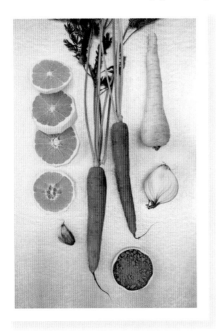

Turmeric's healing properties

Turmeric, a relation of ginger, has long been used in Chinese medicine to help treat depression. It is a natural antiseptic and anti-bacterial agent. However, it's the anti-inflammatory properties that may be of the most interest – they may help arthritis sufferers, soothe inflammatory skin infections such as psoriasis, and according to one study help to reduce the incidence of Alzheimer's.

Superfoods: carrots

Studies have shown that a diet rich in carotenoids (the pigment that makes carrots orange) may help lower the risk of heart disease, while the soluble fibre that carrots contain can help lower blood cholesterol. Their high level of beta carotene is converted by the body into vitamin A and helps maintain good eye health and the ability of our eyes to adjust quickly to changes in light. In traditional medicine, carrots were known for their detoxifying properties and for helping to beat acne. For those trying to keep wrinkles at bay, vitamin A is thought to nourish the skin and help fight the signs of ageing; it is even added to some beauty creams! But before you overdose on carrot juice, bear in mind that too many carrots can make your skin turn a little orange.

Grape nutrient-booster

Naturally sweet grapes are a terrific way to disguise the taste of nutritious veg such as cabbage in a juice. As the pumpkin seeds in this drink are finely ground, no one will know they are there either!

Serves 1

* 2 pears, halved
* ¼ small Savoy cabbage, roughly chopped
* 1 tbsp pumpkin seeds
* 150 g/5½ oz green seedless grapes
* small handful of crushed ice (optional)

Whizz it up

Feed the pears and cabbage through a juicer. Put the pumpkin seeds in a blender and whizz until finely ground, then add the grapes and crushed ice (if using) and whizz again. Pour in the pear juice mix and whizz until smooth. Pour into a glass and serve immediately.

Cabbage nutrition

You may have heard about the seven-day cabbage diet to help you detox and shed weight, but you may not know that Savoy cabbage (part of the same family as kale, Brussels sprouts and broccoli) has long been a favourite in herbal remedies. Savoy cabbage is a storehouse of phytochemicals and powerful antioxidants, which are thought to help protect against cancer. It also contains a huge range of vitamins and minerals, not to mention beta carotene and the amino acid glutamine (an anti-inflammatory). Plus it may help to reduce bad cholesterol in the blood.

Seed swap

Don't have any pumpkin seeds? Then add
a few sesame or sunflower seeds or a small
handful of finely ground almonds instead.

Index